"Who Says Your Fantasies Can't Collide With Your Reality?"
Monica Victoria

Contents

"Who Says Your Fantasies Can't Collide With Your Reality?"   1

Fullpage image   2

Chapter 1   3

Chapter 2   6

Chapter 3   11

Chapter 4   16

Chapter 5   19

Chapter 6   21

Chapter 7   23

Epilogue   25

Fullpage image   27

Fullpage image   28

"Who Says Your Fantasies Can't Collide With Your Reality?"   29

"Who Says Your Fantasies Can't Collide With Your Reality?"

Chapter 1

Echoes of Loss

Jessie Ann sat at her usual corner table in the dimly lit diner, her petite frame hidden by the oversized booth. her tousled, long brown hair hanging over her shoulders as her green eyes focused on her own thoughts. The smell of fresh, brewed coffee and warm pancakes filled the air, but she was lost in a fantasy world of her own, gazing out the window at the bustling streets of New Orleans. The vibrant colors and lively music seemed distant, overshadowed by the echoes of her past. At age twenty-one, she had become an expert in pretending that everything was fine, yet her heart felt like a fractured mirror, reflecting pieces of joy and sorrow that refused to fit together.

Losing her entire family in that devastating car accident had left her sadly adrift. Her mother, her father, and her older sister had been everything to her, her whole world. They were her guiding lights in a dark world that often felt faint and chaotic. Now, at the diner, she merely served coffee and various kinds of pies to patrons who barely even noticed her. It was simply a dead-end job, but it kept her afloat.

Each day, Jessie Ann clung to her dreams, her fantasies of a life where she was truly loved, noticed, where she was whole again.

A Little Diner in New Orleans...

Nestled on a quiet corner of a cobblestone street in New Orleans' French Quarter, a small diner radiates the charm of a bygone era. Its weathered brick facade, painted a soft shade of teal, catches the light of the setting sun, giving it an almost magical glow. The neon sign hanging above the doorway flickers to life as dusk falls, spelling out "Mama Ruby's" in warm, cursive letters, accompanied by the hum of the fluorescent tubing.

The moment you step inside, the scent of Creole spices and fried catfish envelops you, as though the air itself has been seasoned. The mere scent of fresh coffee and bacon swirling through the air in the early morning light. The interior is cozy, with just enough room for a dozen red vinyl booths that line the walls. A scattering of mismatched chairs surrounds a few small tables in the center, their surfaces gleaming despite the years of use. A long counter stretches across one side of the room, its laminate top worn smooth, with chrome barstools standing ready for regulars to reclaim their spots.

The decor is a love letter to the city itself. Faded jazz posters, antique mirrors, and black-and-white photographs of brass bands are tacked to the walls. A pair of Mardi Gras beads dangles from the edge of a shelf holding an eclectic collection of coffee mugs, each one chipped but cherished. Behind the counter, a small chalkboard lists the day's specials, written in a looping hand: gumbo, jambalaya, shrimp po'boys, and a pecan pie that everyone swears is the best in the city.

A jukebox in the corner hums quietly, playing old blues tunes that seem to resonate with the soul of the diner. Fats Domino's voice croons softly over the clink of silverware and the gentle murmur of conversation. The staff, clad in aprons embroidered with the diner's name, moves with an easy rhythm, as though they've been performing this dance for decades.

At the heart of it all is Mama Ruby herself, a stout woman with a quick laugh and an apron smudged with flour. Her presence is magnetic, her voice a soothing mix of honeyed drawl and booming authority as she calls out orders and teases her regulars. She greets everyone with the warmth of a long-lost friend, her eyes crinkling as she insists on refilling your sweet tea before you've taken your last sip.

The food, as unassuming as it appears, is a revelation. The gumbo is rich and smoky, brimming with shrimp, sausage, and tender chicken. The po'boys, overstuffed with crispy fried oysters, practically melt in your mouth. And then there's the pecan pie—warm, gooey, and topped with a dollop of freshly whipped cream, it tastes like a slice of heaven.

Outside, the sounds of the city carry on: the distant wail of a trumpet, the occasional rumble of a streetcar. But inside this little diner, time slows down, and the world narrows to the comfort of good food, warm company, and the enduring spirit of New Orleans.

This is where Jessie Ann spent most of her time...

Chapter 2

The Night That Changed Everything

It was on a sultry summer evening, while Jessie Ann wiped down a counter at the diner, that she first laid eyes on Jacob. He entered the vacant diner with the confident ease of someone who belonged to the city. Tall, with tousled black hair and an easy smile, he was the kind of guy who seemed to draw people in without even trying. Jessie Ann felt a strange flutter in her chest, a swirl of butterflies within her stomach, and a weird mix of hope and fear.

Jacob became a regular at the little diner, stopping by after his shifts at the bar, where he worked in the French Quarter.

Jessie Ann and Jacob exchanged many fleeting glances, casual banter, but she kept her heart locked away. The mere thought of losing someone that she would allow herself to get close to was almost unbearable to think of. So, she built her inner fantasies around Jacob… daydreams where they would wander the exciting streets of New Orleans, laughing and dancing under the moonlight, free from the chains of grief.

In her mind, Jessie Ann let go of all her fears. She imagined a vibrant festival unfolding before them, a kaleidoscope of colors, music, and energy that seemed to pulse in time with her heart. Jacob would take her hand, his fingers warm and strong, as they navigated the crowded streets. The air would be thick with the smell of powdered sugar from freshly made beignets and the rich aroma of jambalaya simmering in cast iron pots. In her daydreams, the chaos of the city became a backdrop to their connection, a perfect harmony of two souls.

As they walked, she imagined them stumbling upon a tucked-away jazz club, the kind of place you only find by accident. The band inside would play the kind of music that made your soul sway, a sultry blend of saxophones, trumpets, and an upright bass that hummed through the wooden floors. Jacob would flash that crooked smile of his, the one that always sent her heart racing, and pull her onto the makeshift dance floor. They would move together, their bodies speaking a language of trust and playfulness. In that world, Jessie Ann had no walls, no fears—just a boundless sense of joy as Jacob spun her around in the dim light of the club.

Sometimes, her fantasies would shift, and she'd picture quieter moments with Jacob. The two of them would sit on a wrought-iron balcony, overlooking the lively French Quarter below. She imagined the scent of blooming jasmine filling the night air as they shared a bottle of wine, their laughter mingling with the distant melody of a street performer's violin. In these dreams, Jacob would listen to her in a way no one else ever had, his eyes never leaving hers. She would tell him about her childhood, about the little quirks that made her who she was, and he would soak up every word like they were precious treasures.

On rainy days, her fantasies turned cozier. Jessie Ann pictured the two of them caught in a sudden downpour, dashing into an antique bookstore for shelter. They would shake off the rain, laughing as droplets fell from their hair, and browse the dusty shelves for hidden gems. Jacob would tease her about her love for old poetry books, and she would poke fun at his fascination with detective novels. In her mind, they would find a quiet corner with a mismatched pair of armchairs and sit for hours, sharing passages from their discoveries, their voices mingling like an intimate duet.

The longer she indulged in these daydreams, the more vivid they became. One day, she imagined a weekend getaway, where Jacob would whisk her away to the Louisiana countryside. They would rent a small, charming cabin near the bayou, complete with a porch swing that creaked softly as they sat together, watching the fireflies dance in the twilight. Jacob would light a fire in the hearth, and they'd spend the evening wrapped in a blanket, trading secrets and sipping hot chocolate. In this dream, Jessie Ann could almost feel the rough texture of the knitted throw against her skin and hear the gentle crackling of the fire as it illuminated Jacob's features.

Some fantasies were grander still. In her mind, Jacob became her partner in adventures she'd only read about in novels. She imagined them boarding a paddle steamer, gliding down the Mississippi River as the sun dipped below the horizon. They would lean against the railing, the wind tugging at her hair, as he whispered stories about the stars. Or perhaps they would explore the haunted corners of the city, daring each other to step into eerie, abandoned mansions and inventing ghostly tales to spook themselves. Jacob's presence in these dreams was always her anchor, his laughter the steady rhythm that kept her grounded.

But there were tender, raw moments in her fantasies too, the kind that made her chest ache with longing. She often imagined a moonlit night on the banks of the Mississippi, the two of them sitting on a blanket spread over the grass. The world would fall silent around them, save for the gentle lapping of the river. Jacob would trace patterns on her palm, a thoughtful look on his face, before finally asking her about the fears she kept hidden. In her daydreams, Jessie Ann found the courage to open up, her words spilling out like a flood, met with Jacob's unshakable understanding.

She even imagined mundane, everyday scenarios that felt like treasures because they involved him. They would cook dinner together in her small kitchen, bumping elbows and laughing as they tried not to burn the gumbo. Or they'd spend lazy Sunday mornings in bed, tangled in soft sheets, sharing stories about dreams they'd had during the night. Jacob would read the newspaper aloud, his voice turning even the dullest headlines into a performance, while she pretended to care, focusing instead on the sound of his voice.

But always, there was a bittersweet edge to her fantasies, a thread of melancholy that reminded her they weren't real. For every imagined kiss under the city lights, every whispered word of love, Jessie Ann felt the weight of her own fear. What if she let Jacob in, only to lose him like she had lost others before? What if the connection she dreamed of so vividly was snatched away by life's cruel unpredictability?

Despite her hesitations, her fantasies continued to grow, each one a world she could retreat to whenever her heart felt too heavy. In these dreams, she wasn't Jessie Ann, the woman afraid of loss—she was a version of herself who had dared to love, to embrace the risk in exchange for the joy Jacob seemed to promise.

As they exchanged glances in the real world, Jessie Ann found herself wondering: could she ever make these dreams a reality? Could she allow herself to take his hand, to let the walls she'd built around her heart crumble piece by piece? The thought was both thrilling and terrifying. Until she found her answer, she clung to her fantasies, savoring every stolen moment with Jacob in the vibrant world she'd crafted in her mind.

Chapter 3

A Dangerous Game

Though, fantasies had a way of actually colliding with one's reality...

One evening, as she served Jacob coffee, he asked her to join him for a drink after her shift was over. Jessie Ann hesitated. 'What if he saw her brokenness? What if he realized that she was just a waitress in a diner with issues, with mere fantasies, about wanting to know him closer? What if he sensed she was lost and merely alone?' she thought, as these questions swirled in her mind, but something in his fragile, kind eyes urged her on, and against her better judgement, she accepted with a smile.

Later that night, Jacob and Jessie Ann sat in the lively bar where Jacob was often employed. The bar was filled with jazz music and faint laughter. Jessie Ann found herself laughing with Jacob, as they talked about silly subjects. The walls around her heart were slowly crumbling, and it frightened her. Jacob shared many childhood stories of his life, and Jessie Ann found herself revealing small pieces of her own, merely skipping over the gaping holes of her loss, only focusing instead on the dreams that kept her afloat these days.

With each passing moment, the fine line between fantasy and reality blurred in her mind, until they felt like one and the same. Jessie Ann had never known such a connection with someone other than her sister, so, this was frightening. Jacob seemed to be everything she had been longing for, yet her mere fear of actually loving him loomed heavy in her chest.

Jacob leaned back in his chair, his face alight with a mischievous grin. "Okay, Jessie Ann, you're going to love this one. So, when I was about eight, my family went camping for the first—and last—time ever. My dad thought it'd be great for us to bond with nature, you know? Except, he had no idea how to pitch a tent."

Jessie Ann chuckled, imagining a young Jacob fumbling in the wilderness.

Jacob continued, gesturing animatedly, "We finally got the tent up after what felt like hours—by which I mean Dad yelling instructions while my mom and I tried to make sense of the mess of poles and fabric. That night, it started raining, and guess what? We'd pitched the tent in a dip in the ground, so it flooded. My mom woke up to water pooling under her sleeping bag, screaming about leeches."

Jessie Ann burst out laughing, the image of chaos and soggy sleeping bags vividly forming in her mind.

"Oh, it gets better," Jacob added, grinning. "In the morning, we discovered we'd accidentally set up camp about twenty feet from a public hiking trail. We weren't in the middle of nowhere; we were essentially on display for everyone walking by."

Jessie Ann shook her head, wiping tears of laughter from her eyes. "That's terrible—but hilarious. Did your family ever go camping again?"

Jacob shook his head solemnly. "Nope. That was the end of the great outdoor experiment. My dad sold the tent at a garage sale the next month.

The night unfolded with similar stories, each one revealing more about Jacob's personality—his humor, his resilience, and his surprising tenderness. He spoke of his misadventures with his siblings, the time he accidentally set the kitchen curtains on fire while attempting to make grilled cheese, and the summer he tried to build a treehouse, only for it to collapse because he hadn't used proper nails.

Jessie Ann found herself laughing more than she had in years. With each story Jacob shared, she felt an inexplicable warmth radiating from him. It wasn't just his words but the way he told them, the way his eyes sparkled with genuine amusement as he relived his past.

And then, in a moment of rare openness, Jessie Ann found herself sharing one of her own stories.

"I used to dream of being a dancer," she said softly, her fingers tracing the rim of her glass. "My sister and I would put on little performances in our living room for my mom. She always said we could be on Broadway someday."

Jacob's gaze softened. "You still dance?"

She shook her head. "Not anymore. Life kind of... got in the way."

Jacob leaned forward. "You should. I mean, I don't know much about dance, but I can tell you light up when you talk about it. I bet you're amazing."

His earnestness caught her off guard. Jessie Ann quickly looked away, the vulnerability of the moment almost too much to bear. Yet, deep down, she felt the faintest flicker of hope—like maybe, just maybe, her dreams weren't entirely out of reach.

As the night wore on, Jessie Ann realized something extraordinary: Jacob was different. He wasn't just kind; he had a way of making her feel seen, as though he wasn't judging her for the pieces of herself she kept hidden. She could talk to him without fear, even as she carefully sidestepped the deeper scars of her past.

Jacob's voice softened as he shared a more poignant memory. "When I was twelve, I used to build these little wooden boats with my grandpa. He'd always say, 'A good boat is like a good life—it needs balance and care.' I didn't really understand what he meant back then. But after he passed, those words stuck with me."

Jessie Ann nodded, the gravity of his words settling between them. "It sounds like he was a wise man."

"He was," Jacob said, his voice tinged with nostalgia. "And stubborn. He once made me rebuild a boat because I'd rushed through it. Said it wasn't about the end result—it was about taking the time to do it right."

Jessie Ann felt a lump form in her throat. "Sounds like he taught you a lot."

Jacob smiled, a touch wistfully. "Yeah, he did."

With each passing moment, the fine line between fantasy and reality blurred in Jessie Ann's mind, until they felt like one and the same. Jacob seemed to be everything she had been longing for: someone who could make her laugh, who understood her silences, who didn't demand more than she was ready to give.

But this newfound connection also terrified her. Jessie Ann had never known such intimacy with anyone other than her sister, and the idea of truly opening herself up to Jacob was almost paralyzing. What if he saw the full extent of her brokenness and decided she wasn't worth the effort?

And yet, as Jacob recounted another tale of his childhood—this one involving a botched science fair project that resulted in a school evacuation—Jessie Ann couldn't help but laugh again, her fears momentarily forgotten. She realized that, for the first time in a long while, she wasn't thinking about her past or her pain. She was simply in the moment, enjoying the company of someone who made her feel alive.

The bar began to empty as the night wore on, and the jazz music softened to a slow, dreamy melody. Jacob glanced at Jessie Ann, his eyes full of warmth. "I'm glad you came out tonight."

Jessie Ann smiled, her heart pounding. "Me too."

As they walked out into the cool night air, Jacob turned to her. "Jessie Ann, I know we've just started getting to know each other, but... I think you're incredible. You have this light about you, even if you don't always see it."

Her breath caught in her throat. She wanted to believe him, but the weight of her insecurities held her back. "I'm not sure I'm as remarkable as you think."

Jacob reached out and gently took her hand. "Maybe not. But I'd like to find out."

For the first time in years, Jessie Ann felt the stirrings of something she thought she'd lost forever: hope.

Chapter 4

Cracks in the Facade

As Jessie Ann and Jacob formed a small relationship, it seemed to deepen. Jessie Ann wrestled with her inner fears, her mere fantasies within her actual reality. She had created elaborate fantasies of their mere future, where they built an actual life together, yet each false dream was shadowed by her hurtful past. She often caught herself pulling away, sabotaging simple moments of intimacy, merely terrified of the inevitable loss.

One late night, after a particularly close moment, Jacob pulled her aside, "Jessie Ann, what's going on with you lately? You seem distant, even when we are together." His brow furrowed in slight concern.

Jessie's heart raced in her chest. She could not merely tell him the truth, that she was afraid to love him due to losing him, that she was terrified, afraid, to actually let him fully in her heart.

"I'm just... not used to all this..." she replied, forcing a faint smile. "You make me happy, but I do not know how to handle it all."

Jacob studied her, his gaze softening as he tilted his head slightly. "Jessie Ann, happiness doesn't have to be so scary. I know you've been through a lot, that much I can sense, but I'm not here to hurt you."

His words, so gentle, made her chest tighten with an ache she couldn't name. Jessie Ann wanted desperately to believe him, but her mind was a battlefield of memories—harsh words, abandonment, betrayal. Each time she tried to move closer to Jacob, those ghosts whispered, reminding her that love was a fleeting, painful thing.

"I know you're not," she murmured, her voice barely above a whisper. "It's just... I've been hurt before. Letting someone in feels like handing them the power to break me."

Jacob reached out, brushing a strand of hair behind her ear. "I get that," he said softly. "I've been hurt too. But you're not alone in this. We can figure it out together, at your pace."

The sincerity in his voice threatened to undo her. She felt tears prick the corners of her eyes, but she blinked them back, unwilling to let him see how much his words affected her. Jessie Ann wanted to tell him everything—about the nights she cried herself to sleep, about the walls she'd built so high even she couldn't see over them. But the words wouldn't come.

Instead, she nodded, her throat tight. "Thank you," she managed to say, her voice cracking slightly.

Jacob smiled gently. "I'm not going anywhere, Jessie Ann. But I need you to meet me halfway. Can you do that?"

She hesitated, her mind warring with itself. Part of her wanted to run, to hide behind the safety of her walls. But another part, smaller yet persistent, whispered that maybe—just maybe—Jacob was different.

"I'll try," she finally said, her voice trembling.

"That's all I can ask," he replied, taking her hand in his.

The warmth of his touch sent a shiver through her, both comforting and terrifying. Jessie Ann realized that trying meant more than simply staying; it meant fighting the urge to retreat, to self-sabotage. It meant allowing herself to hope, even if hope felt like a risk that she wasn't sure she could take.

As they sat together in the quiet of the night, Jessie Ann felt the smallest crack in her armor. She didn't know if she could fully let Jacob in, but for the first time in years, she thought she might want to try.

Chapter 5

Embracing Reality

As time went on, Jessie Ann realized that she couldn't keep living in mere fear of what may come to pass. Jacob had become her anchor, her friend, pulling her from the mere depths of her inner sorrow. With him, she actually began to rebuild her confidence, her life, piece by piece. She sold her family's house in the bayou, shedding layers of much grief that had clung to her like shroud.

After confessing her past, her pain, to Jacob one evening, Jessie Ann felt a small release, she had no choice but to just let go of her miseries now. Although, she still held on to her inner fantasies, especially about Jacob, she slowly accepted her new reality of life. She slowly let her family of her past go, may they rest in sweet peace.

Eventually, she moved into Jacob's apartment in the French Quarter, a vibrant place, a space filled with bright colors and soft music. It was a small, cozy, two-room dwelling, but it felt like a new start, a new home, and Jessie Ann started to envision a brand-new future that included a lot of love, laughter, and brighter hopes.

She even started 'dancing' again', though it was only in the privacy of their apartment, but it made her feel 'free' in her spirit, much more alive inside in her heart. Some afternoons, Jacob would attempt to dance with her, but he was not very good at it. Jessie Ann would usually end up laughing at him, as he would wrap her in his masculine arms and tell her how much he loved her.

Life seemed to be going easy, between her fantasies of dancing and her reality of being loved once again. She felt she could exhale...

Chapter 6

The Unexpected Surprise

Just as Jessie Ann thought she had found her mere footing within her reality, life threw her a curveball.

She discovered, on late evening, that she was pregnant. The news was overwhelming, but as she stared at the tiny pink line on the pregnancy test, a new fantasy took root in her mind... one that was tangible and filled with much hope. She wanted to be the perfect mother, the perfect parent, and the perfect friend to her child.

Jessie Ann imagined how wonderful it would be to take her child to a park and watch him, or her, play with other children. To see her child run and smile while playing with her father, Jacob, as they chase each other in circles. Between fantasy and her reality, she felt a peace in her heart, that everything was going to be alright, happy.

Jacob's reaction to the surprising news was a blend of excitement and fright, but together they would navigate through the unknown. They would face this thing called 'parenthood' head on and be successful. Jacob wanted a boy, but he would be so grateful for a girl, yet

Jessie Ann envisioned a little girl with bouncing curls and green eyes, a daughter that she would name Angel Marie, who would carry the light of their love into the world as she grew into a respectable, fascinating woman.

The pregnancy was rough, but well worth the struggle. Jacob consistently catered to Jessie Ann's every need. She was happy, but wished it was all over with, yet her fantasizing kept her intact. Her mere fantasies helped her endure through her reality of being pregnant.

Chapter 7

Collision of Fantasies and Reality

The bright day that Angel, her little baby girl, was born marked a major turning point in Jessie Ann's life.

Holding her baby girl in her arms, wrapped in a pastel pink blanket next to her warm chest, was the greatest fantasy of all, the greatest reality of all.

Jessie Ann felt an overwhelming sense of peace, mere joy, and in that moment, all the fractured pieces of her broken heart began to align. As she looked into Jacob's caring eyes, she knew she had found her perfect reality, her mere fantasy had come true... she was loved.

With Jacob by her side, steadfast and loving, Jessie Ann knew, she understood, that she could choose to be truly loved, even amidst the painful shadows of her past. She knew her deceased family would be so proud of her now.

As Jacob, Jessie Ann, and baby Angel Marie settled into their new life, she realized that she no longer needed to escape her inner fantasies now. She had built a new reality that was rich and full, woven with threads of true love and mere joy.

The sweet laughter of her daughter filled the apartment as time moved on, and the soft music of the French Quarter became the mere backdrop of her new life, her new reality.

Many nights, Jessie Ann would sway to the soft music from outside her window, as she held Baby Angel Marie in her arms, as Jacob would smile while he watched them from his chair across the room.

Her reality was becoming her mere fantasy...

Epilogue

A New Dawn

Years later, Jessie Ann watched as Angel Marie twirled in the sun-drenched park, her sweet laughter ringing like soft music in the warm air. The vibrant colors of New Orleans surrounded them, a mere painting to a life that felt whole, complete, filled with much warmth and love.

Jessie Ann turned to Jacob, now her husband, who stood beside her, his masculine hand resting gently on her shoulder. They exchanged a smile that spoke great volumes, a shared understanding of the small journey they had taken together, from heartache to mere happiness.

"Look at her, Jessie Ann," Jacob said, his kind eyes sparkling with great pride, "That is our daughter, and she is perfect."

Jessie Ann nodded in agreement, her heart swelling with gratitude, "She is perfect, Jacob. I never imagined that I could feel this way after everything I lost, after all I had went through."

Jacob took her hand in his, his grip steady and reassuring, "You took the hardest leap, Jessie Ann, you allowed me into your guarded heart, and now your fantasy has become your reality."

"I was so afraid then," she admitted, her voice soft as she smiled at him, "But you showed me that it was okay to love and be loved, even when it felt so risky."

As Jacob and Jessie Ann watched Angel Marie play, and run freely, a burst of joy in her every movement, Jessie Ann felt a rush of great thankfulness. She realized that the fantasies that she once clung to had truly become her reality, they were far more beautiful than she could have ever imagined.

With each passing day, Jessie Ann had built a wonderful, joyful life that embraced both her hurtful past and her bright future, a life where she could finally breathe without any weight of fear.

"Who says your fantasies can't collide with your reality?" Jessie Ann whispered to Jacob, a smile spreading across her fragile face.

"Exactly." Jacob replied, pulling her close in his arms as they both watched their lovely, vibrant daughter spin, run, lost in her own world of wonder, her own fantasies.

In that very moment, Jessie Ann knew that love, like the vibrant city, the mere heart of New Orleans, was alive with much possibility now, as the laughter and the music surrounded them. She was ready to embrace life, embrace it all, every beautiful moment that was yet to come.

The End.

"Who Says Your Fantasies
Can't Collide With Your
Reality?"
By Monica Victoria

I'm Jessie Ann. I'm just a girl who lives in my own fantasy!

Journey with Jessie Ann as she overcomes her struggles of existing and finding Love in her abnormal life!

A tale of heartache, love, and unpredictable fate!

"Who Says Your Fantasies Can't Collide With Your Reality?"

"Who Says Your
Fantasies Can't Collide
With Your Reality?"